All Copenhagen
and North Zealand

Text: Martin Tønner Jørgensen
Photographs: Trojaborgs Forlag A/S

Design, lay-out: Trojaborgs Forlag A/S

Distribution in Copenhagen:
TROJABORGS FORLAG A/S
Tlf.: +45 43 54 58 00
Fax: +45 43 73 70 00
www.trojaborg.com
E-mail: trojaborg@trojaborg.com

ISBN 87-89868-69-2

Trojaborg

INTRODUCTION

The Danes are surrounded on all sides by water. Lakes, rivers, fjords and bays give shape to the profile of the Danish archipelago, and the geography of the city of Copenhagen is a faithful reflection of the physiognomy of the country as a whole.

Standing beside The Sound (Øresund), just a few kilometres across the water from Sweden, water is omnipresent in the Danish capital. Copenhagen grew up around a natural harbour situated between the Zealand (Sjælland) and Amager islands, and the oldest parts of the city are separated by the strait between the two islands.

The medieval quarter looks out over Christianshavn, a district built on the opposite bank in the 17th century, whilst, in their turn, the people of this emblematic quarter have no doubt that the moat of the old fortress draws an indelible frontier with the rest of «Devil's Island», as the Zealanders are pleased to call the Amager part of Copenhagen. To the west, a system of lakes separates the old city from the districts of Østerbro, Nørrebro, Vesterbro and Frederiksberg, which grew up

towards the end of the 19th century, when the city walls were demolished. Here and there, the old bastions have been converted into parks, forming a green belt which begins at the famous Tivoli amusement park and continues through, amongst others, the Botanical Gardens, finally terminating at the

Nyhavn harbour.

Citadel Park (Kastellet). There is always a green area close at hand in Copenhagen where we can take a breather. Or we can sit down by the waterside and dream of voyages over the open sea to strange countries. The parks and the constant presence of water make a great city like Copenhagen a truly pleasant place to visit or to live in.

When summer takes up residence in Copenhagen, bringing nights as short as a pleasant sigh and a dazzling sun during the day, Copenhagen becomes a city of dream, even for the Danes. Then we can get out our bicycles or jump in the car and visit the nearby beaches in Amager or to the north of the city, or simply stroll through the streets, falling in love with a beautiful stranger at each corner. June is the month with most sunshine hours, though August also tends to be a sunny month. July, on the other hand, is the rainiest month of the year. Temperatures are mild, averaging around 17°C in summer, and on the odd occasion when the heat rises to 30°C, the Danes begin to suffer. September brings the autumn, and the parks are decked out in yellow and orange, rain and wind begin to set in, and darkness begins its gradual conquest of the city, heralding in the short, icy days of winter. The poet Henrik Nordbrandt says that a year in Denmark has 16 months, because it is as if there were four Novembers. But, though the autumn and winter months seem never-ending, spring is welcomed in rapturously each year. Visitors from warmer climes will be surprised to see semi-naked Danes sunbathing all over the city when the first warmer days arrive in April. Perhaps this climate of brusque changes is partly responsible for that mixture of joviality and melancholy which marks the national character of the Danes.

The tranquil waters between Zealand and Amager have been used as a base for fishermen since prehistoric times. In the 11th century, the importance of the township of Havn (harbour or port) began to rise due to its privileged situation in

INTRODUCTION

the rich herring fishing grounds of Øresund and the attendant trade. In 1167, Bishop Absalon built a fort on the islet where Christiansborg Castle now stands. This fortress was soon to play an important strategic role in King Valdemar the Great's efforts to increase Danish power in the Baltic Sea against the Germans of the Hanseatic League. Absalon is considered the founder of Copenhagen, which was originally known as Købmændenes Havn (Port of the Traders) and which was later transformed into the city's present name of København.

In 1343 King Valdemar Atterdag installed his government in Copenhagen and proclaimed the city the capital of the kingdom. In those times, Copenhagen lay at the centre of a nation which also included three provinces on the other side of Øresund. From that moment on, in spite of a history plagued by disaster, Copenhagen has maintained its status as the most important city in Scandinavia: in 1658-59, Swedish troops laid siege to the city for months in a war whose consequence was the loss of the three above-mentioned provinces; twice in the 18th century much of the city was burnt down, and Christiansborg Castle was razed to the ground on both occasions; and the city was bombarded for three days by the English Navy during the Napoleonic wars, the first time in history that the civil population had been the target of such an attack.

Though most of medieval Copenhagen was destroyed as a consequence of wars and fires, the city still conserves an enormous wealth of Renaissance buildings, the legacy of the great «Builder King», Christian IV, whose long reign from 1588-1648 was, nevertheless, disastrous. However, despite the many military defeats he led his country into, and his constant draining of the national exchequer, to the desperation of the Danish people, Christian IV now enjoys a privileged place in the national memory. To him we owe countless buildings and even entire neighbourhoods. There can be no doubt that without Christian IV Copenhagen would have been a much less interesting city. Another king, Frederik V, also left the city a considerable legacy in the form of the aristocratic district around the Amalienborg Palace, built during his reign. Later, in 1848, Frederik VII granted the country its first democratic constitution, opening the doors to a modernising air which caused the profound transforma-

tion of Copenhagen, which now has a total population of 1.5 million between the city and its vast suburbs. Some people believe that the new bridge over Øresund will lead to the extension of the metropolitan area of the city on the other bank, bringing about a de facto "reunification", between the capital and its former province of Skåne (Scania).

A century after the king's death, the great poet Johannes Ewald used the legend of Christian IV in composing the national anthem. Ewald was the first of a string of important writers living in Copenhagen, three of whom in particular have found a place in universal literature. Hans Christian Andersen (1805-75) wrote his immortal tales, loved

Copenhagen Harbour (Langelinie). Above: Monument to Bishop Absalon, the founder of Copenhagen, in Højbro Plads.

by the young and not-so-young all over the world, in his house in the Nyhavn district of the city. His contemporary, the philosopher Søren Kierkegaard, hardly left the city in the 42 years of his life, but his ideas have had a decisive influence on 20th-century thinking. Finally, Karen Blixen is more famous for the farm she owned in Africa, but nevertheless wrote practically her entire oeuvre in a mansion in the north of Copenhagen. The city has also produced many great names in the world of natural science, from the Renaissance astrologer Tycho Brahe, to H. C. Ørsted, who discovered the laws of electromagnetism in 1820, and the physicist Niels Bohr, contemporary and rival of Albert Einstein. In our days, great

footballers of the category of a Michael Laudrup or a Peter Schmeichel were formed by Copenhagen clubs.

Though the Danish capital owes its existence largely to the herring of Øresund, this tasty fish is now practically impossible to find in the waters of the strait. Nonetheless, herring continues to enjoy pride of place in the local cuisine, and is one of the most popular dishes in the many typical restaurants found all over Copenhagen. Smoked and, above all, salted, «sild» is an indispensable element in the great Danish «frokost», a seemingly never-erending meal made up of a series of hot and cold dishes. Herring is served to accompany «schnapps», a powerful liquor of which various

types exist: «Rød Ålborg», real fire water, is the most typical, whilst «Brøndum» and «Jubilæum» are not so strong. Other delicacies never lacking from the menu of a frokost are «frikadeller», meat balls fried in butter with red cabbage, and plaice fillets with remoulade sauce. The entire repast is served with black bread and abundant quantities of beer. Another typical ingredient in Danish cuisine is «smørrebrød», a slice of black bread with butter and cold meat, vegetables or fish in surprising combinations. All the best restaurants serve smørrebrød a la carte, cooked to order. Finally, there are hot dog stands on practically every street corner of Copenhagen. In Denmark hot dogs are served with ketchup, mustard,

ØRESUNDSBROEN

The bridge across the sound (tunnel, bridge, and artificial island), which connects Denmark with Sweden, was opened by the Danish Queen Margrethe and the Swedish King Carl XVI Gustaf on the first of July 2000. The tunnel is 4.050 metres long and connected to the artificial island, which is 4.055 metres long.

The bridge, which is the longest cable-stayed bridge in the world for road- and rail traffic, is 7.845 metres long. The high-level bridge, which is 55 metres above water level, is 1092 metres long and has pylons of 204 metres (the highest structure in Sweden).

Traditional Danish dishes.

remoulade sauce, fried or raw onion and jerkins, a strange mixture, perhaps, but one many come to appreciate.

A Danish frokost is best served on a hand-painted plate from the Royal Porcelain Factory (Den Kongelige Porcelænsfabrik), whilst drinks should be served in glasses from the Holmegaard glassworks. Both companies, which represent the finest of Danish arts and crafts, turn out both articles for everyday use as well as more artistic creations. Another example of the quality applied arts produced in Denmark are the silver works of Georg Jensen. Nonetheless, probably the most highly appreciated of the country's craft industries is based on its great tradition in furniture design, famed all over the world. The functional chairs designed by the architect Arne Jacobsen, «The Ant» and «The Egg», are veritable cult objects nowadays. Another great success of Danish design are the cold and elegant hi-fi systems produced by Bang & Olufsen.

Two examples of Danish arts and crafts: jewellery made from amber and ceramic pieces.

Overall view of Town Hall Square (Rådhuspladsen).

TOWN HALL SQUARE

Town Hall Square (Rådhuspladsen) is the nerve-centre not just of the city of Copenhagen, but of all Denmark. This is where Kilometre Zero is located, and the sound of the bells of the Town Hall tower ringing out at noon every day to mark the beginning of the national news programme is unmistakable to all Danes, young and old alike. This is the largest square in the city and the place chosen by the locals to express both their indignation and their joy. Over 100,000 people gathered here to celebrate the liberation from German occupation in May 1945, and the square was filled once more decades later, when all Denmark seemed to gather to wel-

come home the triumphant national football team after its victory in the 1992 European Championship, proudly displaying the trophy from the balcony of the Town Hall.

The present town hall is the sixth to be built for the city government. Various of the preceding buildings were burnt down, but the gigantic fortress inaugurated in 1905, the work of architect Martin Nyrop, seems to be gifted with immortality. This mixture of Nordic modernism with touches from Northern Italian styles is, above all, imposing. The central room, 1,500 square metres in size, is equally grandiose. The room is used as a polling station and for cultural events. The Town Hall Wedding Room is famous for its decoration, the work of painter

Joachim Skovgaard. Another of the attractions of the building, always open to the public, is the world clock designed by Jens Olsen: this timepiece, located on the ground floor, has 13 synchronised mechanisms to allow it to tell the time all over the planet. For its part, the 110-metre high tower commands fantastic views over the city. Town Hall Square has been altered on several occasions in recent decades. Traffic from various parts of the city converges here, and the square is also the main hub of the city bus service. The present organisation of the square successfully resolves this complex urban space, with a large pedestrian area in front of the Town Hall, whilst traffic is diverted along the sides of the square. Nonetheless, a modern building which serves as the bus terminal has caused great controversy, as some are concerned that it breaks completely with the historic ambience of the square, whilst others argue that the city has to evolve architecturally. This austere, black building was under the threat of demolition for many years, but seems over time to have won its place in the square.

Dragon Fountain (Dragespringvandet).

Details from the decoration of the Town Hall (the coat of arms of Copenhagen).

Clock of the World, designed by Jens Olsen.

The shopping street called "Strøget".

STRØGET

«Strøget» is a promenade formed by a series of streets and squares crossing the whole of the old city of Copenhagen. It begins in Town Hall Square and ends in New King's Square (Kongens Nytorv), covering a distance of 1,600 metres, making Strøget one of the longest pedestrian streets in Europe. The principal activity of those who walk the Strøget is shopping, for the promenade is lined by shops of all kinds. Football fans can find their favourite team's shirt next to a shop selling select items of jewellery made from amber, whilst young shoppers can pick up cut-price jeans elbow-to-elbow with ladies exploring designer furniture shops. Copenhagen's four most important department stores also have establishments in the immediate vicinity of Strøget.

The first section of Strøget, **Frederiksberggade**, links Town Hall Square with the twin Old and New Squares (Gammeltorv and Nytorv). This is the gateway to the city centre for people coming from the nearby Central Station and is, therefore, a busy street, where strolling tourists mingle with the more business-minded locals walking at a more decided pace. We may also bump into the occasional cyclist here, breaking the traffic rules (many of Copenhagen's cyclists are rather anarchic in their behaviour). This bustling street is also a good place to note, if we had not already, that not all Danish women are blond and not all Danes have blue eyes. Here we find young people whose roots may be found in the plains of Anatolia or refugee camps in south Beirut but who chat together with the strongest of Copenhagen accents.

The back streets north of Frederikberggade once formed the Latin Quarter of the city, a site of doubtful reputation. But nowadays Larsbjørnsstræde, Skt. Pedersstræde and Studiestræde, which intersect with Frederiksberggade, are streets lined by fashionable shops and small but select restaurants and bars. Nevertheless, the district has still conserved its cheerful, friendly atmosphere. Back on Frederiksberggade, near Old Square, is the place where the philosopher Søren Kierkegaard was born and lived for many years. The house is no longer there, but a memorial plaque indicates where it once stood.

Old Square and **New Square (Gammeltorv and Nytorv)** form a single space broken only by Strøget. The first, as its name indicates, is the oldest square in Copenhagen. Once the centre of the medieval city, the tiny market which regularly takes place here has roots marked

The Fountain of Charity.

Amagertorv - here you will find Illums Bolighus, Royal Copenhagen and Georg Jensen.

STRØGET

by over 800 years of the history of trade. In the centre of the square is the **Fountain of Charity**, which once supplied the city with drinking water carried here along wooden water channels from Lake Emdrup, five kilometres away. Until the great fire of 1795, Old Square was presided over by the first town hall, built in the 15th century. Fire razed most of the old houses in the centre, which were replaced by a series of neo-classical constructions giving this area an austere yet elegant touch. An example is the great building, adorned by pillars, which dominates New Square. This was originally built as the new seat of the local authorities, but now houses the Copenhagen Courthouse. Taking Nygade and Vimmelskaftet streets, we come to the heart of Strøget, **Amagertorv** Square, with the **Fountain of Storks** (Storkespringvandet), a popular meeting-

Helligsåndskirken.

Amagertorv. Fragment from the Stork Fountain. "Quick-shaw".

Photos from "Strøget" and Amagertorv. Below: Højbro Plads.

place. This funnel-shaped square opens up on one side to another pedestrian street, **Købmagergade** («Traders' Street»), and on the other to **Højbro Plads** («High Bridge Square»), which leads to the islet occupied by Christiansborg Castle. At the narrowest part of Amagertorv is the **Helligåndskirken** (Church of the Holy Spirit), one of the oldest religious buildings in the city and, all which remains standing of a great monastery pertaining to the Order of the Holy Spirit. Chesslovers meet opposite this church to play matches in the street.

The building at number 6, Amagertorv was built in 1606 in Dutch Renaissance style. This splendid house is the seat of the **Royal Copenhagen**, an umbrella institution including, amongst others, the Royal Porcelain Factory, the Georg Jensen silver works and the Holmegaard glass works. The building houses an exhibition of the best of Danish art and craft work which the public can admire before moving on to the shops.

The last section of Strøget runs through **Østergade**, where the department stores Illum and Magasin have their establishments. Just a block away from Østergade is the **Nikolaj Kirke** (Church of Saint Nicholas). The church tower is medieval, whilst the nave was built in the early-20th century. The building

Thorvaldsens Museum is situated on the Islet of Christiansborg at the canal.

is no longer used as a church, but is an exhibition centre with a most pleasant cafeteria. Østergade and its immediate vicinity is also where we find the city's most traditional bars, obligatory stop-offs on the so-called «death route», a happening or pub-crawl involving journalists, artists and intellectuals and which, nowadays, is more myth than reality, though the bars continue to provide pleasant ports of call.

A part of Gammel Strand, a street overlooking the waters around Christiansborg Castle. As this statue of a fish vendor reminds us, Gammel Strand was where fishmongers once sold their wares.

In Gammeltorv, we take Nørregade to visit the Church of Our Lady (Vor Frue Kirke). This church was founded in the early-13th century, but the original building was razed to the ground by fire in 1314. A second construction was also destroyed, this time in the English naval bombardment of 1807. The current building, in Neo-Classical style, was constructed between 1811 and 1829 and is attributed to C.F. Hansen. Since 1929, the date when island of Zeeland was divided into two dioceses, it has been the Lutheran cathedral of the capital. On 14 May 2004 Vor Frue Kirke was the setting for the marriage ceremony of the heir, Prince Frederik, and Mary Donaldson. On the façade, the tympanum is decorated with a bronze relief by Bertel Thorvaldsen, also the artist of the large Christ presiding over the grand altar, the baptismal font in the form of an angel carrying a conch shell, and the statues of the apostles in the central nave.

Our Lady, the Cathedral of Copenhagen (Vor Frue Kirke).

Thorvaldsen Museum, with artworks from this celebrated Danish sculptor, born in Copenhagen in 1770. The museum itself was financed in a large part fin by Bertel Thorvaldsen, although he did not live to see it finished, as it was inaugurated four years after his death in 1848. The building is by M.G. Bindesbøll, who was inspired by Greco-Roman antiquity. The main façade is composed of five large porches and is crowned by a bronze quadriga, a work from H.V. Bissen. A frieze which runs along the other three façades show us the life of the sculptor and the establishment of the museum. Thorvaldsen rests below a simple granite slab in the interior patio. In addition to many works by Thorvaldsen, the museum brings together paintings from great Danish and European painters of the era.

Christiansborg Castle. Equestrian statue of Frederik VII, the author of the Constitution.

CHRISTIANSBORG, THE OLD STOCK EXCHANGE AND THE CHURCH OF HOLMEN

One of the streets which encircles Christiansborg Castle is **Gammel Strand** (Old Beach), though one would have to dig rather deep to find the sands of this old beach in the very heart of the city of Copenhagen. The names live on, but the landscape has changed considerably since, in the mid-12th century, Bishop Absalon decided to build a fort on an islet near the township of Havn. Of the waters which once protected the medieval fortress from the coast, only narrow Frederiksholms Kanal (Channel of the Islet) remains, and the street Holmens Kanal has been paved for centuries. In **Højbro Plads** (High Bridge Square) is an equestrian statue of Bishop Absalon dressed in armour, guarding the original gateway to the islet, but of the fortress he built all that remains are the ruins of the walls in the basement of the present Christiansborg Castle. Absalon's stronghold was destroyed by the soldiers of the Hanseatic League in 1369. Just a few years later, another was built, extended on several occasions until 1731, when Christian VI decided to build a real palace in the French style, giving it the name of **Christiansborg** (Christian's Castle). But this palace, too, was razed to the ground, this time by the great fire of 1794, and of the original building only the **hippodrome** remains standing. The second Christiansborg was completed in 1828, but was burnt to the ground once more 50 years later, though the church was saved this time. The present castle dates from 1928, since when the fire brigade has, at last, been allowed some peace.

Whilst it is perfectly fitting that a statue of the warlike medieval bishop should guard the entrance to the

CHRISTIANSBORG, THE OLD STOCK EXCHANGE AND THE CHURCH OF HOLMEN

castle from Højbro Plads, it is equally appropriate that an image of the country's first constitutional king, Frederik VII, should watch over the entrance to Christiansborg. Soon after his coronation as an absolutist monarch in 1848, Frederik VII was challenged by a rebellion in Copenhagen, inspired by the revolution in Paris, a revolt which he handled in his own way. It is said that the king waited impatiently for the arrival of a deputation of the rebels in order to give in to all their demands for democracy. A parliament was elected just a few months later, and within the year Denmark had its first constitution, peacefully agreed, and the king could devote more time to his great love, archaeology.

Christiansborg continues to be the seat of political power in Denmark, for the castle houses the three most important constitutional institutions. Several ministries, including the Prime Minister's Office, have their seat here, and one of the castle wings houses the Supreme Court. The rest of Christiansborg is occupied by the **Parliament** or Folketinget («People's Congress»). The Parliament buildings are open to the public and, when not in session, visitors can see the Plenary Chamber, the Senate (now abolished) and the famous bar, or «Snapstinget» («Schnapps Congress»), where many a political agreement will no doubt have been reached.

The royal family has lived in the Amalienborg Palace since the fire of 1794, but the **Royal Reception Chambers** are in Christiansborg. Official audiences take place in the **Throne Room** which, as its name suggests, contains the physical throne of the kingdom. Queen Margrethe II no longer sits at it, however, but uses a more comfortable chair for her work. In another room, the **Council of Ministers**, she meets members of the government to sign laws approved by Parliament. Christiansborg occupies the greater part of the Islet of the Castle, but there are also several other interesting buildings here. The **museum devoted to the sculptor Bertel Thorvaldsen** and the **Tøjhusmuseet** (War Museum), are found here, for example (see the chapter on the museums

Aerial photo of Copenhagen. To the left: The Stock Exchange and Christiansborg Castle. To the right of the canal: the Church of Holmen.

Two views of the old stables in Christiansborg Castle, now converted into a museum.

War Museum (Tøjhusmuseet): cavalry uniform.

of Copenhagen). Another institution we can visit here is the **Royal Library**, overlooking the waters of the port, which has just been extended by the addition of a striking building known popularly as the «Black Diamond».

Beside this example of modern architecture is one of the jewels of Renaissance Copenhagen, the

The arsenal (Tøjhuset) was built between 1598 and 1604 by Christian IV to supply the entire Danish and Norwegian fleet. Later, in 1734, it passed into the possession of the army and, finally, in 1838, Christian VI converted it into a military museum. In the photo, view of the Tøjhuset and the monument to Chancellor Peder Griffenfeld.

View of the former Stock Exchange tower, crowned by a spire formed by the interwoven tails of four dragons.

former **Stock Exchange** (Børsen), built by order of Christian IV. Like other works promoted by this tireless «Builder King», the Stock Exchange was built according to the canons of art, and was completed in 1620. Five years later, the building was completed by the addition of a tower and the impressive spire formed by the interlacing tails of four dragons. The building operated as the stock exchange until 1974.

Strangely enough, **Holmens Kirke** (Church of the Islet) is not on the island itself, but stands on the other side of the channel, opposite the Stock Exchange. The church was inaugurated in 1619, also during the reign of King Christian IV, as the Naval Church, fittingly housed in a building where anchors were made. Denmark's greatest naval

Royal Library - the building is called "The Black Diamond".

HOW TO GET AROUND IN COPENHAGEN

If you want to become acquainted with Copenhagen in an alternative way, you have different means of transport at your disposal.

Try the regular harbour bus with stops at some of the major attractions like romantic Nyhavn and the Opera House. The harbour bus stops at 5 different points, one of them being the Royal Library, and the whole tour only takes 18 minutes. See www.hur.dk

If you prefer a city tour, various sightseeing busses offer their services, among them Open Top Tours, a double-decker departing from the Town Hall Square and from Langelinie, and on its way it passes more than 35 tourist attractions. For more information see www.sightseeing.dk

It is great fun for 1 or 2 persons to try a "Quick-shaw" bicycle taxi. You will find them at squares like Amagertorv/Strøget and Kultorvet/Købmagergade.

In the centre of Copenhagen you will also find free bikes: the City Bike "Bycyklen" is available for use from more than 100 bike stands by inserting a coin of 20 DKK in a slot. The coin is returned when the bike is returned to a stand. A unique service!

CHRISTIANSBORG, THE OLD STOCK EXCHANGE AND THE CHURCH OF HOLMEN

heroes are buried in the church, including the most famous of all, Peder Wessel, better known by his warlike noble title of Tordenskjold (Thundershield). Like other famous Danes, the writer Ludvig Holberg, for example, Tordenskjold came from Norway, until 1814 a Danish province. He won fame in the wars against Sweden, the eternal enemy in the early-18th century, cunningly outwitting enemy admirals on more than one occasion.

Fragment of the altarpiece of Abel Schröder.

Church of Holmen.

CHRISTIANSHAVN
AND HOLMEN

Halfway between the islands of Zealand and Amager, the Christianshavn (Christian's Port) district still conserves its unique personality. Founded, needless to say, by Christian IV to reinforce both the defensive system and the trade of Copenhagen, Christianshavn was built in the early-17th century on various islets in the strait between the two islands. From the old city, we take Knippelsbro, named after a former city councillor, to reach Christianshavn. On the left of the old bridge is the seat of the **Ministry of Foreign Affairs**, an imposing building, but something of an oddity in this gentle city due to its severe appearance. A much more artistic building is the **Church of Our Saviour** (Vor Frelsers Kirke), which presides over the district with its peculiar but most attractive snail-shaped spire. Visitors can take an outer staircase to go up to the top of

Christianshavn Canal.

CHRISTIANSHAVN AND HOLMEN

Christianshavn Canal.

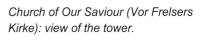
Church of Our Saviour (Vor Frelsers Kirke): view of the tower.

this tower, though this is not recommended for those who do not have a good head for heights. Nonetheless, those who do brave the climb up to the golden dome which crowns the spire will be rewarded by fantastic views over the whole of Copenhagen and much of the Island of Amager. Near the church is the **Navy Museum** (Orlogsmuseet), which houses collections of weapons, artillery pieces, uniforms and several models of boats.

Until just a few decades ago, Christianshavn was a rather unsafe area. Now, however, the charming atmosphere created by the many canals which criss-cross the district has begun to attract both companies and well-off individuals, and the old buildings are being restored. Many of the picturesque houses which line the veritable backbone of the district, the Christianshavn Canal, have been standing since the times of Christian IV, creating a unique ambience, with shops, bars and boats, above all many boats. The king's love of all things Dutch can be noted in most of his works, but perhaps nowhere else did he manage to transfer the charm of Holland to the Danish capital as in Christianshavn. The whole district has an air reminiscent of Amsterdam not only in its urban layout and buildings, but also in the free-thinking, somewhat anarchic personality of its inhabitants. Generations of alternative movements have found refuge here, particularly since the foundation of **Christiania**.

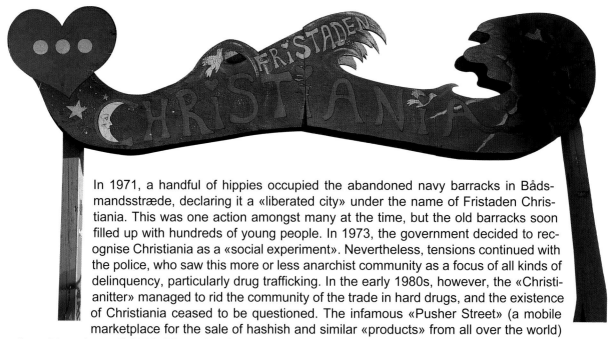

In 1971, a handful of hippies occupied the abandoned navy barracks in Bådsmandsstræde, declaring it a «liberated city» under the name of Fristaden Christiania. This was one action amongst many at the time, but the old barracks soon filled up with hundreds of young people. In 1973, the government decided to recognise Christiania as a «social experiment». Nevertheless, tensions continued with the police, who saw this more or less anarchist community as a focus of all kinds of delinquency, particularly drug trafficking. In the early 1980s, however, the «Christianitter» managed to rid the community of the trade in hard drugs, and the existence of Christiania ceased to be questioned. The infamous «Pusher Street» (a mobile marketplace for the sale of hashish and similar «products» from all over the world) continued to exist until 2003. The sale of marihuana is illegal, but is more or less tolerated by the police, which limits its action to the occasional raid. Pusher Street area is, without doubt, the most striking part of Christiania, but there are other places of interest. There are various restaurants here, for example, including one of the highest category, as well as two concert halls. Moreover, the workshops and studios of Christiania conserve many traditional trades and offices: we find a factory turning out handmade bicycles here, for example, or an expert in the restoration of steel heaters.

Views of Christiania.

In the north of Christianshavn, right on the border with the «municipal borough» of Christiania, is the bridge communicating it with **Holmen** («the Islet»). Holmen is a string of artificial islands used for centuries to form Denmark's main naval base. In recent decades, however, the navy has gradually transferred its administration, schools and docks to other bases, and part of its land here has now been given over to civil use, propitiating the formation of a new and fascinating district of Copenhagen.

Most of the buildings in Holmen have been declared national monuments. Nonetheless, this does not prevent Holmen from being a dynamic part of the city, full of students by day and pleasure seeking folk at night. Many institutions offering training in different artistic trades, such as the Denmark Film School, the State Theatre School, the Royal Academy of Architecture and the Rhythmic Music Conservatory, have all moved to Holmen. This is also where we find some of Copenhagen's most fashionable restaurants and bars, housed in the huge, unusual spaces provided by, for example, the unit where submarines were once repaired or the old cannon store. The latter has now been converted into a restaurant serving up to 700 customers.

Figure-head from Holmen.

The old hoist in Holmen, once used to lift the heavy masts onto boats, and the Battery of Sixtus, from where salutes are fired at Royal Visits.

HOLMEN

Copenhagen Opera House

Europe's most modern Opera House is situated in Copenhagen. A family foundation owned by the largest industrial concern in Denmark, the A.P. Møller-Mærsk Group, donated the newly built Opera House to the Danish State in October 2004, and on January 15, 2005 the Royal Theatre of Copenhagen had its opening performance of opera and ballet here.

The Opera has a unique location on the waterfront of the Dock Island in the inner harbour facing Amalienborg Palace, the residence of Queen Margrethe II.

The Copenhagen Opera House is designed by one of the most outstanding Danish architects, Henning Larsen. The front part of the complex contains a foyer and auditorium for the public; behind there are an experimental stage with seats for 200 guests, rehearsal rooms for chorus, musicians, singers and dancers as well as dressing rooms, workshops and offices.

With its six stages, the Opera has the possibility of presenting an ample repertoire of opera and ballet, and the great auditorium with 1,641 seats is acknowledged to have superb acoustics.

The decorations are made by prominent Danish artists; Per Arnoldi has designed the stage curtain as well as the logo for the opera, Per Kirkeby has created the four large bronze reliefs in the foyer, and the three light sculptures over the bar zone, plan 1 of the foyer, are works by Olafur Eliasson.

One of the typical yellow houses of Dragør and the harbour of Dragør.

DRAGØR

Dragør, an old village of fishermen and sailors which has conserved its traditional air, lies on the southern coast of the island of Amager, near Copenhagen Airport. In the old part of the village, around the harbour, the centuries seem to have passed by unnoticed. The tiny yellow houses stand shoulder to shoulder and the narrow, cobbled streets follow an unusual, rather haphazard urban pattern.

The settlement has existed since the Middle Ages, when it sprang up thanks to the herring fishing trade in Øresund. In the early 16th century the village suddenly grew due to an initiative of King Christian II, who brought in 200 families of Dutch immigrants to cultivate the fertile lands of Amager. This injection of Dutch blood can still be noted in the surnames and traditional costumes of the island folk, many of them on display in the Dragør Museum. The old village has now become practically a residential district of nearby Copenhagen.

Not far from Dragør is a huge green area covering the entire western part of the island of Amager. Part of this land was once used by the artillery for target practice, but all of it has now been converted into a nature reserve with a network of bicycle tracks. A walk through the fields of Amager, amongst cows and other farm stock, allows us to completely forget for a time that we are just a few minutes from a large city. On the other side of the island are the nearest beaches to the centre of Copenhagen. The old «Helgoland» baths, a wooden construction standing in the sea, are a veritable architectural jewel.

Exterior view of the Round Tower. To the right above: Our Lady and the Round Tower. Below: the ramp leading up the Round Tower.

RUNDETÅRN
– THE ROUND TOWER

At the end of the pedestrian area of Købmagergade («Traders' Street») where it crosses with Strøget, stands one of the most peculiar buildings in the whole of Copenhagen. With the Little Mermaid, the Rundetårn (Round Tower) is, without doubt, Copenhagen's best-loved symbol. Once again, we owe this monument to King Christian IV. The Rundetårn forms part of the Church of the Holy Trinity (Den Hellige Trinitatis Kirke). However, it is not a belltower, but it was designed for the study of the stars. The king's idea was to create a scientific and religious complex made up of a church for the spiritual education of its students, a university library and an astronomi-

cal observatory. The tower began to be built on 7 July 1637, Feast of the Holy Trinity, and was completed five years later. An inscription in gold at the highest point of the tower façade perfectly expresses the pious desire of the Danish monarch: «That God may let true teaching and the sense of justice into the heart of King Christian IV, 1642».

Honestly speaking, Rundetårn is not a particularly attractive building. With a height of 34.6 metres, it cannot be said, either, to be one of the most monumental works in the city. Much of its power of attraction lies, without doubt, in its extraordinary spiral ramp. A total of 209 metres in length, this ramp twists seven and a half times around the tower until it reaches the observatory. Few children have been able to resist enter-

ing the Round Tower by racing up to the top, and few can have failed to dream of riding a bicycle down the ramp. That this element is an open invitation to play was amply proven by the Russian Tsar Peter the Great when he visited the Rundetårn in 1716. Peter rode a horse up to the top of the tower and, even more admirably, was followed by a carriage bearing the Tsarina Jekatarina. The top of the Rundetårn commands good views of the old part of the city, though these can only be appreciated through the bars of a grille installed to deter suicides. The observatory was used by the University of Copenhagen until 1861, and the old telescope is still installed here. The observatory is opened to the public one day per year, allowing visitors to gaze at the stars with the aid of this instrument, light years from the possibilities offered by modern technology.

The original church was partly burnt down in 1728, though, fortunately, the tower was spared. The present building dates from 1731. The church attic was used as a university library until 1861. In 1987, however, its doors were opened once more after restoration, and the space is now used as an exhibition centre and auditorium for classical music concerts.

Beside the entrance to the Rundetårn is a bust of the great Danish astronomer Tycho Brahe, installed here many years after the reign of Christian IV, for the old king would most certainly not have liked to see this physicist presiding over this tower. In fact, Tycho Brahe was forced to flee from his observatories on the island of Hven in Øresund due to disagreements with Christian IV. The famous astronomer died in Prague in 1601, exiled by the king who, ironically, 40 years later, made the Round Tower a monument to the study of the stars.

Overall view of the interior of the church.

The crowns of the Danish monarchy.

Rosenborg Palace.

ROSENBORG

If Christiansborg personifies austere power and Amalienborg contained elegance, what is expressed by the smallest of Copenhagen's castles, the Rosenborg Palace, is pure exuberance and extravagance. The palace, completed in 1634, was built as a place of recreation then outside the city walls by Christian IV. Like most of the works undertaken by this king, the style of this tiny palace takes its inspiration from the Dutch Renaissance. Rosenborg, perhaps, marks the point of maximum refinement in this tendency, and is further set off by the idyllic park, known to the people of Copenhagen as Kongens Have (King's Garden). Rosenborg means «Castle of the Rose», and Christian IV was enchanted by his «floral» palace, residing here for long periods, and dying in this, his favourite palace, in 1648. Later monarchs chose other palaces for their periods of rest, and the last king to live in Rosenborg was Christian VII, who took refuge here from an English attack on the city in 1801. In 1833, the palace was converted into a museum, a function it still performs today.

Danish monarchs were never exactly Sun Kings but, judging from the rooms in Rosenborg, they would have liked to have been. The great Knights' Room, on the second floor of the palace, was used by Christian V, a contemporary of Louis XIV of France to receive audiences. The room is presided over by the throne used for his investiture as crown prince, and is a fine work of narwhal tusk and ivory. Three silver lions guard the throne of Christian V, the same king who

Rosenborg Palace.

ROSENBORG

installed a mirror room in imitation of Versailles on the first floor. Most of the rooms in Rosenborg are dedicated, with paintings and personal effects, to the different kings and queens of Denmark since the reign of Christian IV, occupying several rooms on the ground floor and ending with the last king of the Oldenburg dynasty, Frederik VII. The rest of this Chronological Collection of the Danish Monarchs is to be found in Amalienborg. In the basement at Rosenborg are the royal insignias and the Danish crown jewels which were kept in a safe to which only the monarch had a key until 1922. Rosenborg Park – Kongens Have – is a much-loved spot for the people of Copenhagen. At the first sign of good weather this, the most central of the city's green spaces, is immediately filled by people taking the sun, enjoying a picnic on the grass,

The Gardens of Rosenborg (Kongens Have) with the statue of the Queen Caroline Amalie.

The Rosenborg Palace features many apartments decorated with great pomp. In the photo, the Ceremonial Room.

ROSENBORG

The Great Knights' Room, presided over by the throne used by Christian V at his investiture as crown prince. Guarded by three silver lions, the throne is made of ivory.

drinking a beer or simply strolling along the different paths. Beside Rosenborg Palace are the barracks of the Royal Guard, Den Kongelige Livgarde, which keeps watch over the royal residences. The changing of the guard takes place daily, the soldiers marching to the accompaniment of a band along Gothersgade towards Amalienborg, escorted by traffic police.

Rosenborg: clock.

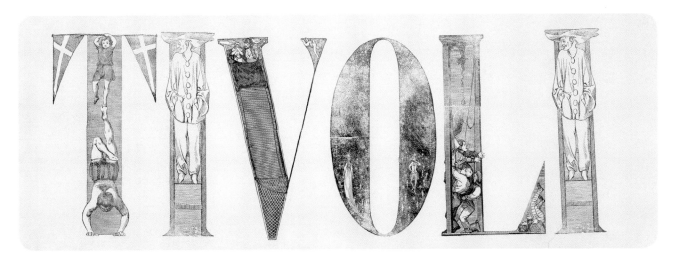

TIVOLI

The Tivoli Gardens, which house one of the oldest amusement parks in the world, lie between Town Hall Square and Copenhagen Central Station. However, those who frequent Tivoli call it «the old garden», and they are quite right, as the site has little to offer by way of a funfair. There are a few of those diabolical machines which take visitors up, down and round about before returning them, dizzy, to earth, but not many. Most of the attractions, like the Switchback or the Big Wheel, are more interesting for their structure than for the excitement of the rides they provide. The Tivoli Gardens are, more than anything, an ideal place for a stroll, to have a beer or organise a «frokost», to enjoy a concert or show or to watch the night-time fireworks displays. All this, accompanied by the unique atmosphere of Tivoli, with its myriad flowers and over 100,000 lightbulbs illuminating the night.

Tivoli first opened its gates in 1843 when it stood just outside the still fortified city. Georg Carstensen, an enterprising Dane who loved to travel, had been greatly struck by his visits to funfairs in Italy, England and Germany, and applied for permission to build one in Co-penhagen, but the local authorities were not keen on the idea, fearing that the attractions might exalt the spirit of visitors. Finally, Carstensen managed to obtain an audience with King Christian VIII. At it, he explained that, on the contrary, Tivoli would help people forget politics. It is not known whether the king allowed himself to be persuaded due to the revolutionary fervour which then ran amok throughout Europe or if he simply had the good sense to see the possibilities for enjoyment if such a park was built in the city, which had little in the way of distraction. However this may be, the fact is that Carstensen was granted permission to build his Tivoli, and the funfair enjoyed instant success amongst the people of Copenhagen, and is still enormously popular today.

Of the park Carstensen built all which now remains is the artificial lake. The main entrance in Vesterbrogade and the Pantomime Theatre were built in 1874. In any case, Tivoli conserves its air of days gone by. The Nimb and the Chinese Pagoda cultivate a romantic exoticism, but the garden is, nonetheless, Danish to the marrow. The musical guard wear uniforms in the national colours, red and white, and their bearskin helmets are replicas of those worn by the Royal Guard at Amalienborg. The Pantomime Theatre still puts on performances of ballet, pantomime and «commedia dell'arte», featuring the classical characters Harlequin, Columbine and Pierrot. This last has always been a favourite with children, and the popular tradition at the end of each performance of this silent theatre to shout out «Say something, Pierrot», a request which is always happily granted.

But not everything in Tivoli has an air of the past, for pop and rock music concerts are also organised on the Lawn, «Plænen», and the Tivolis Koncertsal (Tivoli Concert Hall) is one of the most popular in the city.

THE BOTANICAL GARDENS AND OTHER PARKS IN COPENHAGEN

The Botanical Gardens, which lie practically adjoining busy Kongens Have, is one of the most peaceful places in Copenhagen. Whilst the park around Rosenborg Castle is filled with the noise of picknickers and strewn with sunbathers, the nearby Botanical Gardens, on the other side of Øster Voldgade street, enjoys almost absolute peace and quiet. This is the perfect place to take a breather and just sit for a while without distraction unless, of course, one wants to study the plants in this internationally re-nowned collection. The gardens were planted between 1871 and 1874 to assist university botany studies and also served initially for the provision of medicinal plants for pharmacies. The great greenhouse in the centre of the gardens was donated by J. C. Jacobsen, patron of the arts and science and founder of the Carlsberg brewery. Here, in what is the closest we can get to a Danish jungle, grow palms and other tropical plants. The grounds of the Botanical Gardens also contain the botany and geology museums. Like other parks in Copenhagen, the Botanical Gardens were established on land forming part of the bastions in the old city walls.

From here, we can walk on to **Østre Anlæg** (East Park) and then the **Kastellet** (Citadel) park, practically without stepping outside the green area. The characteristic zigzagging forms of ramparts and moats have been conserved in Østre Anlæg, whilst another park built on the site of a former bastion is the **Ørstedsparken**, a little to the southwest of the Botanical Gardens, a popular meeting-place named after the great physicist H. C. Ørsted.

The Palm House of the Botanical Gardens.

Page 43: The statue of H.C. Ørsted in the Ørstedsparken.

GRUNDTVIG CHURCH

found all over the country. These, Romanesque or Gothic in style, are a distinctive feature of the Danish landscape, almost always perched on a hilltop. Few churches in this style are found in Copenhagen, but it seems more than fitting that this element of architectural heritage should have been revived precisely in the church built in homage to N. F. S. Grundtvig.

Niels Frederik Severin Grundtvig (1783-1872) was a priest, poet and politician. He is not as famous as Hans Christian Andersen or Søren Kierkegaard outside Denmark, but his influence on Danish culture is enormous. Grundtvig was the ideologist behind the popular movement which transformed the country through co-operativist ideas and the education of the rural population. He also wrote many psalms and formed his own movement within the Danish church, one based on an open idea of Christianity, opposed to more obscurantist tendencies. The film «Ordet» («The Word»), Carl Theodore Dreyer's masterpiece, narrates the tensions between Grundtvig's followers and those of the Internal Mission (Indre Mission) in a small village.

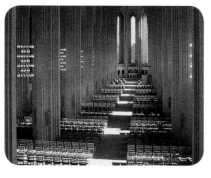

GRUNDTVIG CHURCH

Grundtvig Church (Grundtvigs Kirke) may have the shape and form of a village church, but its size is more that of a cathedral. The tower stands 50 metres high and the nave is 22 metres long. Up to 2,000 people can be accommodated in this great edifice, built of hand-moulded yellow brick. The church, which lies in the peripheral district of Bispebjerg in the northwest of the city, is also installed with a huge organ. In designing Grundtvig Church, completed between 1921 and 1940, architect P. V. Jensen Klint took his inspiration from the old rural churches

View of Kongens Nytorv (New King's Square), presided over by the equestrian statue of Christian V.

KONGENS NYTORV – NEW KING'S SQUARE

New King's Square (Kongens Nytorv) was conceived from the first as an aristocratic space in contrast to the more practical Town Hall Square (Rådhuspladsen). The construction of the square, which elegantly communicates the old city with the wealthy residential districts around the Amalienborg Palace, was completed in 1688 during the reign of Christian V. In the centre stands an equestrian statue of the king, surrounded by a small ovalshaped garden.

The square is flanked by several interesting buildings, the oldest of them the baroque **Charlotten-**borg Palace, completed in 1677. It owes its name to Queen Charlotte Amalie, wife of Christian V, who had her residence here. This imposing building is now the seat of the Royal Academy of Art, a school for painters and sculptors. Every year, the Royal Academy organises the Spring Exhibition, one of the most important art shows in Denmark.

Adjoining Charlottenborg is another building devoted to art, the **Royal Theatre**. The present building was completed in 1874 to replace the original theatre, built in 1748. Whilst awaiting planned extension work, opera singers, orchestra musicians, actors and dancers share the tiny facilities of this building, with its two theatre halls. The best-known com-pany internationally is the Royal Danish Ballet, and choreographer August Bournonville's classical repertoire continues to be popular both in Denmark and abroad, but the company can also court controversy, as it did in the early-1970s with its performances of the ballet Dødens Triumf (The Triumph of Death), dancing completely naked and accompanied by psychedelic music. Two statues preside over the theatre entrance: on the right is Ludvig Holberg, Denmark's most important Enlightenment writer, the author of mordant comedies which are still popular even today; and on the left is the «official» poet of Danish Romanticism, Adam Oeh-lenschläger, famous above all for

The Royal Theatre.

Restaurant "Kong Hans" and Charlottenborg Palace.

his nationalist poetry, but also the author of romantic tragedies. Holberg and Oehlenschläger, irony and dream, are the two faces of the national character, keys to understanding the inhabitants of this tiny country. Opposite the Royal Theatre, on the other side of the square, is the **Hotel D'Angleterre**, a 17th-century palace on the corner with Strøget. This hotel is a veritable symbol of all the most select and costly which Copenhagen has to offer. Nearby, in Vingårdsstræde, is one of the city's best restaurants, Kong Hans, which has one star in the Michelin Guide.

Above: Hotel D'Angleterre, and below: the department store "Magasin".

NYHAVN

Nyhavn (New Port) was excavated in the late-17th century to bring the water of the harbour to New King's Square (Kongens Nytorv). There are bars on the ground floors of most of the old houses, painted in different colours, which line this much-loved canal, and for centuries sea salts from the seven seas gathered here to get drunk and fight together. Now, the atmosphere of Nyhavn is much more peaceful, but this continues to be a place full of life at night. By day, nothing can be more pleasant than to sit at one of the many pavement cafés and enjoy a beer whilst admiring the old sailing ships moored along the canal. This was a view Hans Christian Andersen also enjoyed, as he lived for many years at number 18 Nyhavn.

Many of these boats are no longer put to sea, but have been converted into restaurants or houses. There is even a tiny theatreboat («Bådteatret») in Nyhavn. At the canal mouth is the station of the boats which link Copenhagen with the nearby city of Malmö in Sweden.

This circumstance explains the surprising number of wineries in the neighbourhood, for many Swedes come shopping for wine, beer and other alcoholic drinks in Copenhagen, where prices are rather more reasonable.

Overall view of Nyhavn,
or New Port.

NYHAVN

Many sailing boats are moored along the Nyhavn Canal, though many have now been converted into homes or restaurants.

From Nyhavn: The Memorial Anchor, the sightseeing-boat, and outdoor restaurant life.

Amaliehaven and Amalienborg with the Christian IX Palace, the residence of Queen Margrethe and Prince Henrik.

AMALIENBORG AND FREDERIK'S CHURCH (FREDERIKSKIRKEN)

Photo: Lene Åkerlund

In the mid-18th century, King Frederik V decided to mark the third centenary of the accession of the Oldenburg dynasty to the throne of Denmark by the construction of a new aristocratic district in the northeast of the old city. All the most important families in the kingdom were to build themselves palaces in «Frederiksstaden» (Frederik's City) in accordance with the lines laid down in plans designed by the architect Nicolai Eigtved and inspired in the very Vatican City in Rome. Amalienborg Castle was built in the centre of this new district between 1750 and 1754. The Amalienborg site is made up of four identical palaces with their corresponding wings, arranged symmetrically around an octagonal square. These palaces are in French rococo style. The equestrian statue of Frederik V which presides over the square is considered the French sculptor Saly's most outstanding work. Initially, then, as we have said, Amalienborg was built for the nobility, but in 1794, when the royal family was made homeless by the great fire which razed Christiansborg to the ground, the court was transferred to this elegant complex, and since then Amalienborg has always been the official residence of the kings and queens of Denmark. The present ruler, Margrethe II, is the second queen to have reigned over Den-

mark in its thousand-year history as a monarchy. The first, Margrethe I, did so as queen mother under the title she herself invented, that of «lady and mistress, protector of the kingdom of Denmark». And her reign was a happy one, for she forged the Kalmar Union, uniting the sibling countries of Denmark, Sweden and Norway for the only time in history, a period which lasted over one hundred years. Margrethe II was recognised as crown princess thanks to the reformation of the law of succession enacted in 1953, and acceded to the throne in 1972, at the age of 31, on the death of her father, Frederik IX. Since then, the queen has won a place in the heart of her people as a cultivated, artistic and, above all, open, friendly person. Her Christmas message, broadcast every year on Danish television, is followed by practically the entire population, even the least traditionalist of her subjects. Within the limits of her status as a constitutional monarch, Queen Margrethe always slips in some message referring to current affairs, a discrete reminder about some social problem, for instance, and when Queen Margrethe speaks, the Danes listen.

The queen lives with her husband, the prince consort Henrik, in the building southeast of the palace and known as the Christian IX Palace. Thousands of adults and children gather in Amalienborg Square each 16 April to celebrate the queen's birthday, waving flags and cheering in a show of affection. Queen Margrethe acknowledges by coming out onto the balcony with her family

The equestrian statue of Frederik V.

AMALIENBORG AND FREDERIK'S CHURCH (FREDERIKSKIRKEN)

The Royal Guard in Amalienborg Square, in the middle dressed in gala. Above to the right: the fountain in Amaliehaven.

to greet the crowd.

Amalienborg is guarded night and day by the Royal Guard, or Kongelige Livgarde, which has protected royalty since the corps was founded in 1658. Each day at noon, the changing of the guard takes place, the new troops parading through the streets of Copenhagen from their barracks beside Rosenborg Castle, just a few kilometres from Amalienborg. Except when the queen is not in residence, the ceremony is always accompanied by the Band of the Royal Guard. On holidays, the guards wear gala uniform: white crossed swordbelts over a red jacket and blue trousers, not forgetting that essential item,

Amalienborg Square, presided over by an equestrian statue of Frederik V.

Frederik's Church, popularly known as the Marble Church.

Overall view of the presbytery.

the bearskin helmet.

In the plans drawn up by architect Nicolai Eigtved, **Frederik's Church** (Frederikskirken) formed part of the Amalienborg complex. The Church was planned, along with the palace, to form the central axis of so-called «Frederik's City». In 1749, the king laid the first stone of what was designed to be a luxurious rococo building. The amount of Norwegian marble used led to it becoming popularly known as the Church of Marble (Marmorkirken). When Eigtved died in 1754, the building was far from being finished, but work continued until 1770 when Struensee,

the power behind the throne in the early years of the reign of mad King Christian VII, stopped it as a waste of time and money.

Struensee was deposed and beheaded not long after, but the project remained unfunded and the work was left abandoned as a ruin for over a century. Finally, the Marble Church was finished in 1894 thanks to the donation of powerful financier, C. F. Tietgen, founder of the Tuborg brewery. And, though in the end only the lower section was built of marble, the church has conserved its nickname.

The Marble Church is one of the

few in Denmark with a circular ground plan and is by far the largest in the country. Its majestic vault is 30 metres wide and is decorated with paintings of the twelve Apostles. Moreover, the building stands in one of the most select squares in the city, like a little piece of Paris brought to Copenhagen.

HANS CHRISTIAN ANDERSEN

On April 2, 2005, the 200th anniversary of the birth of the world famous Danish fairy tale writer Hans Christian Andersen was celebrated with various events all over the world.

Hans Christian Andersen was born in Odense on the island of Funen (Fyn) to poor parents; already at the age of fourteen he went to Copenhagen to try to realise his dream of a career at the theatre. Without result, he tried as a ballet dancer, an actor and a singer, but at last, he succeeded in becoming a playwright. He wrote several plays and translated a number of foreign plays, but it was his unique fairy tales and novels that brought him great fame in Germany in the 1830s followed by England and America in the mid-1840s, and after that by the world-fame never matched by any other Dane.

The works of Hans Christian Andersen are translated into more than 120 languages, and his fantastic tales are numerous: "The Little Match Girl", "The Princess on the Pea", "The Ugly Duckling", "The Emperor's New Clothes", "The Tinder Box", "The Little Mermaid", "The Steadfast Tin Soldier", "Clumsy Hans", "The Swineherd", "The Nightingale", "Little Claus and Great Claus", "Thumbelina", "The Fir Tree" and "The Flying Trunk" are among the fairy tales which have enchanted generations of children and adults all over the world.

In Odense Hans Christian Andersen's childhood home is a museum. In Copenhagen he lived many years in Nyhavn and from 1848 to 1865 he had three rooms on the second floor at No. 67. All through his life he made many journeys abroad as travelling was one of his great passions. His motto was: "To Travel is to Live".

Like many other famous Danes, Hans Christian Andersen is buried in the cemetery Assistenskirkegården in Copenhagen.

Paper cuts from the fairy tales. Collage by Preben Jensen & Mogens Seested.

THE PORT OF COPENHAGEN AND LANGELINIE

The enormous equestrian statue of Frederik V which presides over Amalienborg Square was donated by a firm of merchants devoted to trading with the Far East. The booming Danish economy in the mid-18th century, which made it possible to build Amalienborg and the Marble Church, amongst other initiatives, was due, above all, to flourishing trade. The East Asiatic Company (Det Østasiatiske Kompagni) ships brought tea, spices and porcelain from the Orient for sale in Europe, whilst other merchant companies enriched themselves in the lucrative triangular trading strategy of selling arms to Africa, slaves in the Caribbean and cotton in Europe. The centre of operations for these businesses was, naturally, the **port of Copenhagen** or, more specifically, the docks to the north of the old city. This is still the centre of local trade operations, though the goods have changed and the ships are no longer based in the old free port of Copenhagen. The flagship of Danish business, A. P. Møller, known in ports all over the world through its shipping company, Maersk, still controls its vast trade empire from these old docklands.

This whole area of the city has undergone complete transformation in a process which began in the late 1980s. The old warehouses have been restored, new buildings of outstanding architectural value have sprung up, and a walk around the historic docks is now a pleasant experience full of points of interest. We can start such a tour, for example, at the **Larsens Plads** dock, its back to Nyhavn. Here, the warehouses have been converted into hotels, restaurants and luxury homes.

From here, we can go on to Amalienborg and the modern park of Amaliehaven, a gift from the company of A. P. Møller which was opened in 1983.

If we now continue towards the **Citadel** (Kastellet), we will enjoy lovely views of the artificial islands of the Holmen on the other side of the strait.

Copenhagen Harbour, Langelinie.

Church of Saint Albans.

Standing out here is the silhouette of the old mast hoist in the historic Holmen naval base. The Citadel is a pentagonal fortification built in 1666 to defend the entrance of the port of Copenhagen. The bastions were demolished in 1892, however, and the Citadel was converted into a fantastic park. Sheep now graze on the old ramparts, whilst a fleet of ducks and swans patrol the waters of the moat. Nonetheless, the barracks in the centre of the fortress are still operational, and access to the ramparts is occasionally closed while the soldiers undergo training exercises.

There are various points of interest around the Citadel, such as the **English Church of Saint Albans**, the **Liberation Museum** (Frihedsmuseet) or the pompous **Gefion fountain**. This represents the Nor-

Three views of the famous sculpture of the Little Mermaid in Copenhagen. The Foundation of Edvard Eriksen.

dic goddess Gefion who, according to the myth, turned her four sons into oxen, using them to pull off a piece of Swedish land which she then threw into the sea, creating the island of Zealand, whilst the hole she made became the great Swedish Lake Vänern.

The **Little Mermaid**, near the beginning of the Langelinie dock, is rather more discreet. Nonetheless, and despite being so small, this bronze statue installed on the bank on a stone, is a famous symbol of both Copenhagen and Denmark in general. The statue represents the principal character in Hans Christian Andersen's tale of the little mermaid who falls madly in love with a human, with tragic consequences. Perhaps the secret of the undeniably enormous success of this figure, the work of the sculptor Edward Eriksen, erected in 1913, lies in its sweet and melancholy grace. The same cannot be said of the vandals who have decapitated the Little Mermaid on several occasions, and the head we now see is a «transplant».

From the Little Mermaid, our tour continues along the **Langelinie** (Long Straight) dock. This is where the great cruisers, more than 200 a year, usually dock. The reward for those who reach the end of this kilometre-long jetty is a kiosk selling rather excellent ice creams. Inspection of the interior section of Langelinie reveals new office buildings and homes, built around the old free port and with such evocative addresses as Indiakaj or Amerikakaj (India Dock, America Dock, etc).

View of the Museum of the Liberation.

The Gefion Fountain.

NYBODER

Nyboder is one of the most singular districts in Copenhagen, not just because of the shameless dark yellow of the rows of small terraced houses we find here, but also because this was probably the first social housing scheme in Europe. Some 600 one-family dwellings distribut-ed into 20 rows into their respective streets were built here from 1631 to 1648 as part of a plan thought up by Christian IV to provide decent hous-ing for navy employees and situated near the Citadel, built by the same king to protect the port of Copenha-gen. The original homes were sin-glestorey affairs, 40 square metres in size, making them fairly spacious for popular housing of the time. The streets were given unusual names, some of which have survived to the present. These include, for ex-ample, Krokodillegade (Crocodile Street), Hjertensfrydsgade (Happy Heart Street) or Krusemyntegade (Curly Mint Street). Only half a row of houses from the original Nyboder is conserved, at Sankt Paulsgade nos. 20-40. There is a small mu-seum here, containing the recrea-tion of a 17th-century dwelling. The other houses have been extended and enlarged by the addition of a second floor. Nevertheless, they still conserve the cheerful, «vil-lage» air characteristic of Nyboder, though these small but charming homes have now become rather expensive.

THE DISTRICTS OF VESTERBRO, NØRREBRO AND ØSTERBRO

When, in 1872, it was finally de-cided to demolish the walls of the fortified city to allow Copenhagen to grow, the city practically exploded. Industrialisation led to huge waves of immigrants from the fields to the city and, in order to accommodate the rapidly increasing population, the districts of Vesterbro, Nørre-bro and Østerbro were built in just a few decades. As their names denote (Vesterbro, Nørrebro and Østerbro mean West Bridge, North Bridge and East Bridge respective-ly) these new working-class areas grew up around the sites of the old city gates. The Broerne (Bridges) districts now form part of the mu-nicipal borough of Copenhagen, but they still conserve their identity and have their own borough coun-cils with power over certain areas. When people cross the system of lakes which once formed part of Copenhagen's defences, they are going «to the city».

Vesterbro lies between two nation-al symbols: the Tivoli funfair and the premises of the world-famous Carlsberg brewery. The district is articulated around infamous Isted-gade, a street which has for years been a centre of prostitution and drug trafficking. Vesterbro is and al-ways has been a bleak part of the city, but it has its charm and, above all, its legends. The poet Tove Ditlevsen, one of the most out-standing women in Danish letters, narrates like no one the miseries and the dignity of this working-class district, where she grew up in the 1920s and 1930s. Later the writer Dan Turèll portrayed the bars and genuine characters of Vesterbro in his popular poems and novels. But this Vesterbro of legend is chang-ing. There are ever fewer bars of ill repute and more and more modern cafés, the awful housing blocks, which once made up most of the housing here, are being rehabilitat-ed and part of the old city slaughter-house is now used for cultural and sporting activities.

Over the years, **Nørrebro** has often been the scene of expressions of social discontent. Working-class to the marrow, protest groups such as

Søpavillonen.

the squatter movement have established bases here. Most of the time, though, Nørrebro is peaceful but very lively. There is a huge variety of bars and more or less alternative shops here, and the presence of many immigrants, mostly from Islamic countries, gives a special touch to this bustling neighbourhood. But Nørrebro also has its oases of peace and quiet, such as the cemetery **Assistenskirkegården**. Here, we can lose ourselves for hours under the shade of the majestic trees, reading the inscriptions on tombstones or looking for the tombs of the famous (Hans Christian Andersen and Søren Kierkegaard, amongst others, are buried here). The banks of the Peblinge Sø and Sortedams Sø are another peaceful site, though at times the traffic of people jogging can become rather heavy. In very cold winters, the lakes of Nørrebro become skating rinks. Søpavillonen, built on the dike between Peblinge Sø and Sankt Jørgens Sø, owes its existence to this sport, for it was built in 1894 for the Copenhagen Skaters' Association. This unusual wooden building, which takes its inspiration from Russian architecture, has now been converted into a restaurant and dancehall for the elderly.

Østerbro, unlike its sibling districts, has always been a middle-class area. Here we find almost suburban houses lining the streets of a quiet district which enjoys a privileged location not far from the beaches nearest to the north of the city and adjoining Copenhagen's largest green belt zone. If the weather is minimally good enough, **Fælledparken** (Common Park) becomes immediately filled by football matches, particularly at weekends. Unlike the nearby **Parken Stadium**, anyone can play in the park. Parken is where both the Danish national team and the most important football club in Copenhagen, F.C. København, play home matches. On the other side of the Fælledparken are the grounds and facilities of the **Rigshospitalet** (Hospital of the Kingdom). Film director Lars von Trier used the powerful effect of these austere buildings masterfully in the filming of his brilliant soap opera «Riget», which dealt with life in a hospital, a real cult series in Denmark.

Denmark's National Stadium "Parken".

A view of Frederiksberg have, spacious gardens adjoining Frederiksberg Castle.

FREDERIKSBERG AND COPENHAGEN ZOO

Frederiksberg is like an island within the Copenhagen city limits which sprang up around the old village of Solbjerg. Even though the district or borough stretches as far as Lake Sankt Jørgens Sø, at the very gates of the old city, Frederiksberg still maintains a certain degree of independence. As far as everyday life is concerned, the boundary between municipal districts is a fiscal one more than anything, and local taxes are rather lower in Frederiksberg than in Copenhagen. Frederiksberg possesses the «dis-creet enchantment of the bourgeoisie», its impressive mansions and aristocratic apartments forming a well-to-do strip of land between the working-class districts of Vesterbro and Nørrebro, though this is also the principal area for the artists of the night. Theatres and cabarets line the avenues of Frederiksberg and, after the show, its bars, some of them veritable jewels going back over one hundred years, soon fill up with thirsty theatregoers. Another attraction in this district, forming part of the city's heritage, are the «Gamle Haver» (Old Gardens) in Pile Allé. As indicated by their name, these are beer gardens full of atmosphere, where the drink flows freely.

The Old Gardens adjoin Frederiksberg Have, a great green space forming a park around Frederiksberg Castle, built as the royal residence of King Frederik IV and completed in 1703. The original park was laid out according to the canons of the French baroque style, but was replanted as an English garden with Chinese touches in around 1800, and has since been conserved as such. A system of canals encircles «Chinaman's Isle», where a small wooden Chinese pavilion has been built. Another interesting feature of the park is the so-called «Swiss

Views from Frederiksberg Castle and from the gardens.

FREDERIKSBERG AND COPENHAGEN ZOO

Pavilion». Visitors can take small boats out onto the canals.

Beside Fredriksberg Castle, on the top of Valby Hill, marking the beginning of the suburbs, is **Copenhagen Zoo**. The tower here, soaring to a height of 43 metres, commands the most panoramic views of the city to be found. On a clear day, one can see as far as the coast of Sweden. The Zoo, which was opened in 1859, is one of the oldest in the world. In recent years, the old facilities have been reformed to improve the animals' living conditions, however. No doubt, the hap-piest animals in this relatively cold climate are the penguins, the sea lions and polar bears, but as far as one can see the elephants are also delighted with life in Copenhagen. Though far from their natural environment and climate, the elephants of Copenhagen Zoo are those with the best reproduction record in captivity anywhere in the world. The most popular animals with the young and not so young, however, are the primates, which live in the 1,500 square metre Tropical Pavilion, alongside the crocodiles and the snakes. The playful chimpan-zees attract vast crowds, especially at feeding time, when they enjoy a lively meal. There is also a Children's Zoo here, where young visitors can see the domestic animals of Denmark, stroke a little goat or ride a pony.

The Copenhagen Zoo.

National Museum: main antechamber.

MUSEUMS OF COPENHAGEN

The National Museum

Some 15,000 years ago, after the last Ice Age, the first hunters decided to settle down and live in the Danish archipelago. The National Museum (Nationalmuseet), housed in a rococo palace near Christiansborg, offers a fascinating opportunity to discover the world of the Danes of yesterday and before. Here we find recreations showing us the life of Flint Age cultures, as well as a display of spring fashion in 1370 BC in the clothing of the famous «Egtved Girl», dressed in a miniskirt. Her surprising state of conservation is due to the fact that she was buried in a peat bog.

The most famous piece in the museum the Sun Chariot (Solvognen), belongs to the same period. A 60 centimetre-long sculpture in bronze and gold, this represents a horse pulling a chariot with a solar disc, and is probably a religious object. The Golden Horns (Guldhornene) owe their fame to an unfortunate occurrence: these fabulous 5th-century pieces were stolen and melted down in 1802, and those we see today are copies. The crime inspired Adam Oehlenschläger to compose a fervently nationalist poem.

The museum also contains a great deal of material pertaining to the Viking Age, including, for example, several rune stones, and there are also collections here illustrating the Denmark of the Middle Ages, the Renaissance and the 18th century. Also fascinating is the collection of Eskimo treasure, one of the most important in the world.

National Museum: The Sun Chariot (Solvognen) and stones engraved with the ancient Scandinavian runic script.

State Art Museum (Statens Museum for Kunst).

ART MUSEUMS

There are many interesting art museums in Copenhagen, of which the **Statens Museum for Kunst**, near Rosenborg Castle, is particularly interesting. As its name indicates, the collections of this State Art Museum are dominated by Danish art, from the 16th century to the present day. The so-called Golden Age of Danish painting, which took place in the 19th century, is richly represented with works by C. W. Eckersberg, Christen Købke and J. T. Lundbye. Most of these are romantic, intimist paintings which take the Danish landscape as their theme. An entire room is devoted to the work of Vilhelm Hammershøi, the most recent master of melancholy art, featuring his oppressive studies of half-open windows and doors, which touch the spirit in a very Nordic way. Modern art is represented by, amongst others, Asger Jorn and Per Kirkeby. There is also an international section in the museum, as well as a large collection of engravings. A recent extension, moreover, created an interesting combination between the original building, dating from 1896 and modern architecture.

Not far from this museum is the building which houses the art collection of businessman **Heinrich Hirschsprung**, and which also focuses on 19th-century Danish painting.

The **New Carlsberg Glyptotek**, known popularly as the Glyptoteket, houses an important collection of ancient art. Egyptian gods, Roman emperors and Greek athletes populate the rooms of this art gallery, which stands beside the Tivoli Gardens and was built in 1888 by Carl Jacobsen, son of the founder of the Carlsberg brewery and, like his father, a great patron of the arts. The Glyptoteket also contains an important collection of French Impressionist art, with works by Monet, Renoir, Cézanne and Degas, whilst other grand masters of world art represented here include Van Gogh and Gauguin. The latter was married to a Danish woman and lived for a time in Copenhagen before going to Tahiti. The museum garden is housed in a greenhouse where palms and subtropical plants grow, and many people come here just to have a coffee and read the paper in this place, full of the magic of the everyday.

Winter Garden of the New Carlsberg Glyptotek.

A lovely view of the Thorvaldsen Museum on the Islet of Christiansborg.

On Castle Isle (Slotsholmen), by Christiansborg, is the **Bertel Thorvaldsen Museum**, dedicated to the artist of the same name, without doubt the most important Danish sculptor of the 19th century. Thorvaldsen lived for many years in Rome, but came back to Denmark in 1838 to a national hero's welcome, an event commemorated by a frieze in the building exterior. Thorvaldsen loved marble, classical forms and large dimensions, and the museum is full of implacable emperors on horseback and gigantic Greek and Roman gods. The thumb of Zeus or Mars can signify a world here. There are also smaller busts in the museum, portraits Thorvaldsen made of rich or famous personalities of his times, as well as works on religious themes. The foundation of the museum was financed by the artist himself and was completed in 1848, four years after his death. Bertel Thorvaldsen is buried in the museum courtyard.

Thorvaldsen Museum: statues of Greek and Roman gods by the Danish artist the museum is devoted to.

Various museums of Copenhagen, among others The Louis Tussaud's Museum with Hans Christian Andersen.

Other museums in Copenhagen

Besides those described above, there is a rich variety of other museums in Copenhagen, offering something for everyone.

The **War Museum** (Tøjhusmuseet) illustrates the history of weapons with Danish examples. Housed in the old Christian IV arsenal on Castle Isle, this museum also features several fine models of warships. Nearby, in Christianshavn, is the **Navy Museum** (Orlogsmuseet), with collections of weapons, artillery pieces, uniforms and a recreation of the captain's bridge of a submarine.

Those interested in the natural sciences will also find plenty to see in Copenhagen. The **Tycho Brahe Planetarium**, at the end of Lake Sankt Jørgens Sø, uses the most modern technology to help visitors understand the mysteries of the stars and planets. The purpose of the **Eksperimentariet**, in Hellerup, in the north of the city, is to teach science through over 300 exhibition pieces and interactive activities. For its part, the **Zoology Museum**, near Fælledparken, is more traditional,

with exhibitions of Danish fauna, as well as an interesting pavilion devoted to the oceans. But the city also offers different opportunities to have fun. Also near Tivoli is Louis **Tussaud's Wax Museum**, which takes its name from a relative of the famous Madame Tussaud, and who sold his name to the Copenhagen enterprise. The museum features wax figures of famous Danish and international personalities.

Another museum, with the un-Danish name of «**Ripley's Believe It or Not**», in Town Hall Square, houses a surprising collection of unusual

The Tycho Brahe Planetarium.

objects. It is at times hard to believe what people will do to get into the **Guinness Book of Records**: a tiny museum in Østergade (Strøget) provides some examples.

Finally, visitors can enter the world, both Danish and at the same time universal, of humorist Robert Storm Petersen, «**Storm P.**», in his small museum in Frederiksberg.

Museum devoted to the Danish humorist Robert Storm Petersen.

Dyrehaven, Palace of Eremitagen and a salon from the palace.

JÆGERSBORG DYREHAVE

The Danish national anthem sings of a lovely country where the beechwoods are reflected in the salty water of the beaches. A romantic image, of course, but one which is a reality in many places, and a particularly apt description of the northernmost area of the Island of Zealand. North of Copenhagen, a string of villages follows coastline of Øresund, some of them well-conserved fishing villages, though most now converted into centres catering to the Danish people's love of sailing. At Helsingør, the strait opens up to the sea, and built-up areas give way to beaches. The inland reaches of the region are dominated by woods and lakes, with villages, farms and no few castles dotted over the landscape. It is no surprise that, in a country where «few have too much and even fewer too little», in the words of the poet N. F. S. Grundtvig, the former æthe richæ live, for the most part, in the townships of North Zealand.

The wood nearest to the city is **Jægersborg Dyrehave** (Jægersborg Hunting Park), which lies just 20 minutes from the centre by train. As its name indicates, this was once a royal hunting reserve. To this end, King Christian VI had the palace of **Eremitagen** built here in 1736. The palace continues to be used for the traditional «Hubertusjagten» foxhunt in the autumn. Nowadays, however, the «fox» is one of the riders and the hunt is, in fact, an obstacle race through the woods. Nor does anyone shoot the 2,500 or so fallow deer, red deer and other cervids in the park. Dyrehaven is now, above all a place to stroll hand in hand under the beech trees on a Sunday, perhaps making a visit to the tiny village of **Raadvad**, which lies beside a lake in the middle of the forest.

Close to the entrance to the wood from Klampenborg station is the old amusement park of **Bakken** (The Hill). The people of Copenhagen have gathered here regularly since 1585, at first to take the holy water from the Kirsten Piil fountain. Over time, taverns and minstrels' shows sprang up around the fountain, taking shape as a funfair about a century ago. Bakken cannot compete with the beauty and grace of Tivoli, but the atmosphere of the village fair has its own special charm. The stands in the park continue to be known as «shops», and in one of them, «Bakkens Hvile», the flame of Copenhagen's minstrel traditions is still kept alive to some extent.

FRILANDSMUSEET (OPEN-AIR MUSEUM)

A visit to the **Open-Air Museum** (Frilandsmuseet) is a journey back in time to rural Denmark. The museum site, in the township of Lyngby, northwest of Copenhagen, forms part of the National Museum. Whilst it is true that many historic buildings have been conserved throughout the country, the Open-Air Museum recreates an atmosphere which has now disappeared completely elsewhere.

The old farmhouses with their characteristic thatched roofs have been dismantled in their place of origin and carefully rebuilt here, brick by brick. Visitors can go into the houses and cottages, whose rooms are installed with the furnishings and domestic utensils typical of their respective periods. The village also contains working pottery, weaving and lace-making workshops allowing visitors to learn about traditional popular arts and crafts. The fields are cultivated using traditional horse-drawn machinery, whilst windmills and watermills complete this scene, depicting the rural landscape of bygone centuries.

The Main Entrance, and a windmill in the Open-Air Museum.

Room in the Karen Blixen's house.

THE KAREN BLIXEN MUSEUM

The park which surrounds the idyllic mansion of Rungstedlund, halfway between Copenhagen and Elsinore, is a long way from the African savannah in more than one sense. Nevertheless, a very direct link exists between the cultivated landscape of North Zealand and the lion country of the Kenyan plains, for it was precisely at Rungstedlund that Karen Blixen recreated her adventures as a hunter and coffee-grower in the book which won her worldwide fame, «Out of Africa», which inspired Sydney Pollack to make his award-winning film of the same name. The writer Karen Blixen was born in Rungstedlund in 1885. In 1914, she followed her husband, Swedish baron Bror von Blixen to Africa, where she stayed on after the couple had separated, running a coffee plantation on her own. When she returned home from Kenya in 1931, she took up residence at Rungstedlund once more until her death in 1962. It was at Rungstedlund that she wrote her entire oeuvre which includes, besides the above-mentioned autobiographical work, a novel and several magnificent collections of stories.

The Karen Blixen Museum was created in 1991, opening its doors to the public that same year. The rooms in the Rungstedlund house are maintained just as she left them, full of mementoes of Africa. The park, which contains a tiny lake and a bird reserve, is also open to the public. Using audiovisual material, the museum tells the story of Karen Blixen's years in Kenya, and visitors can also listen to recordings of interviews and readings by the writer, the Baroness's distinctive grave voice revealing all the eccentricity of this outstanding figure in Danish letters.

THE LOUISIANA MUSEUM OF MODERN ART AND THE ARKEN MUSEUM OF MODERN ART

When an important travelling exhibition of modern art visits Denmark, it normally stops off in the village of Humlebæk, south of Elsinore, for Humlebæk is where we find the Louisiana Museum of Modern Art, an exhibition centre which has carved out an important name for itself in the world of modern art since its foundation in 1958. The core of this internationally-renowned museum is a 19th-century chalet which has been extended on various occasions to form a subtle interchange between modern architecture, art works and the site's magnificent setting, between Lake Humlebæk and the slopes of Øresund coastline. The permanent exhibition at the Louisiana Museum centres on constructivism and the members of the Cobra group, though more recent tendencies are also represented. In the park are sculptures by Henry Moore and Max Ernst, amongst others. The **Arken Museum of Modern Art** (The Ark), opened in 1996, is located between the sea and the port of Ishøj in Vestegnen, a district to the west of Copenhagen. Not all the experts whole-heartedly approve of the extravagant building which houses the Arken collections, designed by the architect Søren Robert Lund, who won the competition to build it whilst still a student. Nevertheless, one must admit that few could remain indifferent to the rebellious forms of the museum, which characterise both the interior and the exterior of the building.

Arken stages exhibitions of Danish and international modern art, with particularly emphasis on the 1940s.

Louisiana Modern Art Museum.

Fredensborg Castle.

Page 79: From the Nordmandsdalen (valley of the Norwegians) with the 69 sandstone sculptures.

FREDENSBORG

The Royal Palace of Fredensborg (Castle of Peace) owes its name to the end of the Great Nordic War in 1720. After centuries of wars against the Swedes, this peace was a blessing, and the opening of Fredensborg in 1722 also marked the beginning of a new period of prosperity for Denmark. This spirit is reflected in the buildings, inspired by the Italian Renaissance architecture King Frederik IV admired so much.

Unlike neighbouring Frederiksborg, just a few kilometres away, Fredensborg is not a castle built with an eye to defence, but a rural palace open to the public. Fredensborg is one of very few of Denmark's most important castles to have entirely escaped damage by fire. The splendid apartments, which are just as they were designed by Frederik IV's architects, can be visited for one month a year, July. For the rest of the year, Fredensborg is closed to the public as it is still a royal residence, much used as such by Queen Margrethe II and her family. Nonetheless, much of the great park which stretches from the palace down to Lake Esrum Sø can be visited throughout the year. The park is designed in French style, with avenues distributed in the shape of a semi-star from the palace towards the lake, and has all the charm, too, of a typical Danish riverside forest. The gardens also contain 69 sandstone sculptures representing Norwegian fishermen and farmers.

FREDENSBORG

Mary and Frederik

The all-important event in Denmark in 2004 was the wedding of His Royal Highness Crown Prince Frederik, 36, and Miss Mary Donaldson, 32, from Tasmania, Australia, which took place on May 14 in Copenhagen's Cathedral of Our Lady.

The Royal Couple met during the 2000 Sydney Olympics and are extremely popular. This popularity became especially evident during their cruise on the Royal Yacht "Dannebrog", in the summer of 2004, taking them to several Danish cities. Their visit to Greenland was also a great success. Crown Prince Frederik has a strong affection for this island since his participation in the famous Sirius Patrol, a sledge expedition for a distance of nearly 2,800 kilometres.

The permanent residences of the Crown Prince Couple are Kancellihuset (the Chancellery House) at Fredensborg Palace, and Christian VII's Palæ of Amalienborg Palace in Copenhagen. They have many representative activities. His Royal Highness Crown Prince Frederik acts as patron of a number of societies and organisations, and Crown Princess Mary has won the hearts of the Danes, because she already speaks Danish very well.

Photo: Steen Evald

Wedding in Our Lady, the Cathedral of Copenhagen.

ELSINORE

Kronborg Castle. Salute in honour of the Royal Yacht "Dannebrog". Below: Sculpture of the mythical hero Holger Danske.

ELSINORE

The fate of Elsinore (Helsingør in Danish) has always been closely linked to its location at the narrowest point of Øresund. When, in 1429, King Erik VII decided to impose a tariff on all boats passing through Danish waters, the tiny fishing village suddenly took on enormous strategic importance. Elsinore was designated as the place where these tariffs were to be paid, and the Gothic houses of the historic centre testify to the prosperity the seaport enjoyed thanks to the trade which came with this activity. In more recent times, the city has become the popular destination of thirsty Swedes, who come here to stock up with beer and other alcoholic beverages, sold here at a rather more reasonable price than in their own country.

But Elsinore's worldwide fame is due, above all, to the great English playwright, William Shakespeare, who set his famous tragedy of the black prince, Hamlet, in its castle. The first fort, Krogen («The Corner»), was built by King Erik to ensure that tariffs were duly paid. In

Views from Kronborg.

ELSINORE

1585, under Frederik II, the Renaissance palace of Kronborg («Crown Castle»), the largest in northern Europe, was built. Destroyed by fire in 1629, the castle was partially rebuilt by Christian IV, who characteristically added various touches of Dutch inspiration. At that time, the cannons of Kronborg also were complemented by those of Kärnan Castle on the opposite side of the strait, ensuring Denmark complete control over shipping passing through Øresund. Nonetheless, the loss of Scania to Sweden in 1658 changed this situation radically, and Swedish troops took advantage of the war to sack Kronborg of many of its treasures. The castle's importance gradually declined until it once more became a centre of attention in the 20th century, this time as a tourist attraction. In the keep at Kronborg is a statue of the mythical hero Holger Danske sleeping. According to legend, he will awaken whenever the kingdom of Denmark is in danger. He has snored on for centuries.

Banqueting Hall of Kronborg Castle.

Photos from the North Zealand Coast.

THE NORTH ZEALAND COAST: HORNBÆK AND GILLELEJE

The beaches at the most northerly point of Zealand are the best in the entire region. In good weather, they are filled by people from Copenhagen, who prefer an hour's drive to the crowded sands of the beaches near the capital. The most popular beaches here are found in the area around the old fishing village of Hornbæk where, as along the entire northern coastline, we find many summer residences which are often used throughout the year.

The constant pressure of the tourist industry has transformed Hornbæk, where fishermen are now a tiny minority. Nonetheless, the village still conserves a pleasant atmosphere and boasts several interesting restaurants.

The nearby village of Gilleleje, on the other hand, still smells of tar. The tiny port is still full of fishing boats, painted, according to tradition, in the lightest blue. Each day, these boats set sail for the fishing grounds of Kattegat, returning with their catches of plaice, cod or monkfish. In the port are fishmongers selling fresh fish, though not necessarily at bargain prices, as tourism has reached these parts, too.

The philosopher Søren Kierkegaard loved the village of Gilleleje, walking the hills of the coast as he attempted to solve some dialectic problem. A monument in honour of this famous visitor stands at the northernmost point of Zealand, Gilbjerg Hoved.

From the beach of Gilleleje. The church, the lighthouse and two views from the harbour.

FREDERIKSBORG

Frederiksborg Slot is, without doubt, Denmark's most splendid castle, standing on three small islands in Lake Hillerød, 35 kilometres from Copenhagen.

There was already a noble mansion here as far back as the Middle Ages. The place was acquired in 1569 by King Frederik II, who converted it into his residential castle. Needless to say, Christian IV was not to be outdone, and demolished practically the entire castle his father had built, in its place creating the fantastic Renaissance palace we can admire today. The castle, completed in 1625, has three wings: the «King's Wing» is in the centre, flanked on the left by the «Chapel Wing» and on the right by the «Princess's Wing». Frederiksborg also features a large courtyard with a great tower guarding the entrance from an unusual S-shaped bridge. The site also contains part of the castle of Frederik II.

Frederiksborg was a royal residence until the construction of the more modern Fredensborg Castle in 1722, but became used as such once more under Frederik VII, who is said to have enjoyed fishing in the lake directly from the castle windows. Under his reign, in 1859, the castle interior was devastated by fire. A national collection, along with an important donation from brewer J. C. Jacobsen, enabled the building to be restored and opened once more in 1878, though no longer as a castle, but as a museum of national history. The original decoration has been restored in some of the rooms, but most of them have been converted to house an important collection of paintings illustrating outstanding events and personalities over the last 400 years of the history of Denmark.

Frederiksborg Castle. The little ferry that sails across the castle lake.

FREDERIKSBORG

Frederiksborg Castle. The Chapel, the Park, the main entrance (the yard with the fountain), and below: aerial photo of the Castle.

Roskilde Cathedral.

ROSKILDE

Roskilde, which lies some 30 kilometres west of Copenhagen, is one of Denmark's oldest cities. This is where we find the tombs of many of the country's monarchs, for majestic **Roskilde Cathedral** contains the pantheon of 20 Danish kings and 17 queens. Margrethe I is buried here, along with all the nation's rulers since 1536, up to the father of Margrethe II, Frederik IX. Bishop Absalon, who also founded Copenhagen, began the construction of the cathedral in around 1170, and work was finally completed about one hundred years later. Two towers were added in the 15th century, crowned by spires by the omnipresent Christian IV in 1636. Although the cathedral was sacked during the Reformation, it still remains the undisputed queen of Danish churches. The Chapel of Christian I contains an unusual column on which the heights of the rulers of 24 different countries are marked. These marks show, for example, that Russian Tsar Peter the Great was 2.08 metres tall, whilst the Danish King Christian VII, at 1.64 metres, was rather shorter.

An even more remote part of Danish history can be seen in the **Vikingeskibshallen**, a museum housing the five Viking boats found in the Roskilde Fjord. These comprise two fast warships and three merchant boats, reconstructed as far as possible and truly impressive to see. The museum also contains full-scale copies which take visitors for boat trips in the fjord.

Roskilde is also an important name for lovers of live music. Some 70,000 people attend the local rock festival, which takes place every year in the first weekend of July.

Views from Roskilde. Above: Vikingeskibs-museet. The Cathedral, houses from the old quarter, and the yachting harbour.

Hendes Majestæt Margrethe II
Hans Kongelige Højhed Prins Henrik

Photo: Steen Evald

DANISH KINGS AND QUEENS

Denmark is the oldest monarchy in the world

Gorm (The Old) . . . . ? - 950	Valdemar II (The Victorious). . 1202 - 1241	Christian IV. . . . . 1588 - 1648
Harald I (Bluetooth) . . . . 950 - 985	Erik IV (Ploughpenny). . . . . . 1241 - 1250	Frederik III . . . . 1648 - 1670
Sweyn I (Forkbeard). . . . . . . 985 - 1014	Abel . . . . 1250 - 1252	Christian V . . . . 1670 - 1699
Harald II . . . . 1014 - 1018	Christopher I. . . . . 1252 - 1259	Frederik IV . . . . 1699 - 1730
Canute I (The Great) . . . . . . 1018 - 1035	Erik V . . . . 1259 - 1286	Christian VI . . . . 1730 - 1746
Hardecanute. . . . . 1035 - 1042	Erik VI. . . . . 1286 - 1319	Frederik V . . . . 1746 - 1766
Magnus (The Good) . . . . 1042 - 1047	Christopher II . . . . 1320 - 1326	Christian VII . . . . 1766 - 1808
Sweyn II (Estridsen) . . . . 1047 - 1074	Valdemar III . . . . 1326 - 1330	Frederik VI . . . . 1808 - 1839
Harald II . . . . 1074 - 1080	Valdemar IV (Atterdag). . . . . 1340 - 1375	Christian VIII. . . . . 1839 - 1848
Canute II (The Holy) . . . . 1080 - 1086	Oluf III (Håkonsson) . . . . 1376 - 1387	Frederik VII . . . . 1848 - 1863
Oluf I. . . . . 1086 - 1095	Margrethe I. . . . . 1387 - 1396	Christian IX. . . . . 1863 - 1906
Erik I (The Kind) . . . . 1095 - 1103	Erik VII (of Pomerania) . . . . . 1396 - 1439	Frederik VIII . . . . 1906 - 1912
Niels . . . . 1104 - 1134	Christopher III (of Bavaria) . . . 1440 - 1448	Christian X . . . . 1912 - 1947
Erik II . . . . 1134 - 1137	Christian I . . . . 1448 - 1481	Frederik IX . . . . 1947 - 1972
Erik III (The Lame) . . . . 1137 - 1146	John (Hans) . . . . 1481 - 1513	Margrethe II . . . . 1972 -
Sweyn III & Canute III	Christian II . . . . 1513 - 1523	
(both claimed the throne) . . . . 1146 - 1157	Frederik I . . . . 1523 - 1533	
Valdemar I (The Great). . . . . . 1157 - 1182	Christian III . . . . 1534 - 1559	
Canute IV (Son of Valdemar) 1182 - 1202	Frederik II . . . . 1559 - 1588	

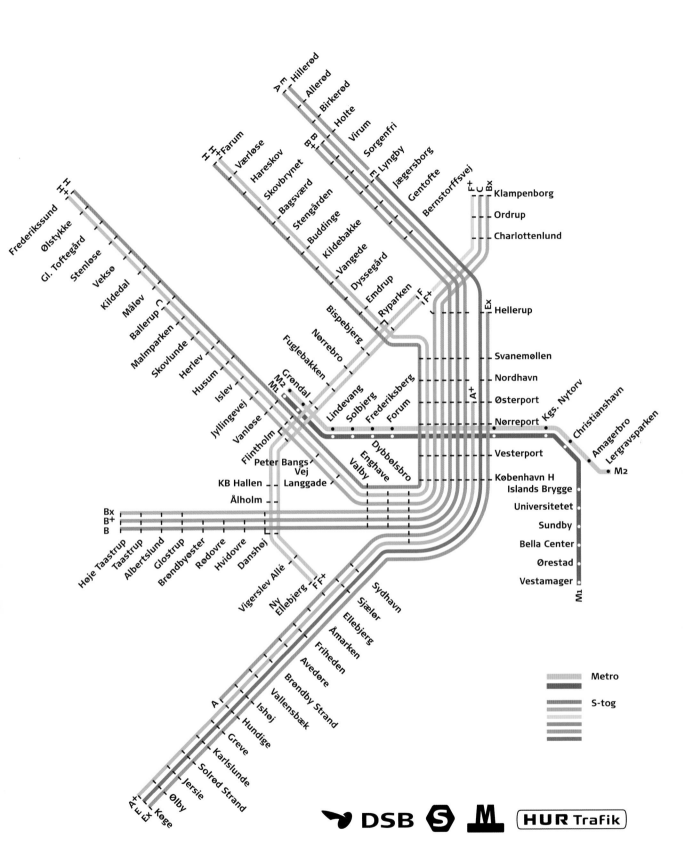

Metro
S-tog

DSB S M HUR Trafik

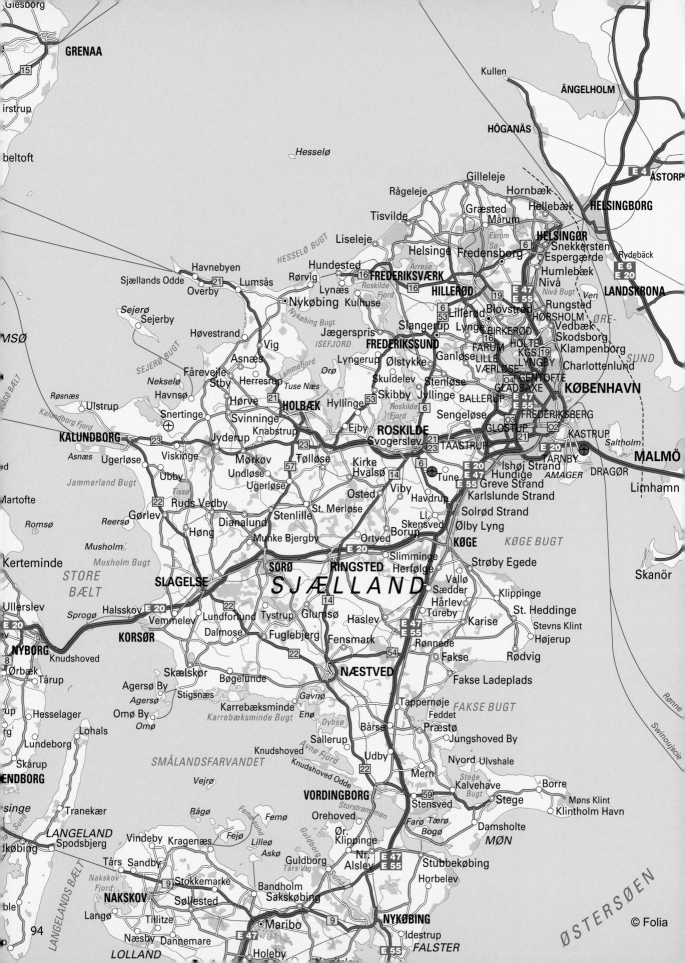